From the humblest of origins Abraham Lincoln rose, through his own unaided efforts, to become President of the United States. He continues to hold a unique appeal, not only for Americans, but for people with democratic principles throughout the world. He is renowned for his personal integrity and his humane personality. But Lincoln's fame rests largely on the fact that his Presidency almost exactly coincided with the duration of the American Civil War.

Although Lincoln led the North in war against the Southern seceding states, his aim was not to abolish slavery in those states, but to save the Union. Later the tide of public opinion, and his own private conviction that slavery was wrong, led him to issue the Proclamation of Emancipation which forever abolished slavery throughout the United States.

Lincoln's relevance in the modern world endures, particularly because of his eloquence as a spokesman for democracy. He believed that the Union was worth saving, not only for its own sake, but because it embodied an ideal of self-government which was, and still is, of interest to the people of the entire world.

The text includes many contemporary quotations, and there is a list of principal characters, a table of dates, a reading list, and an index.

Philip Clark is an author and editor of children's books, and is the author of *Washington* in this series.

WAYLAND HISTORY MAKERS

Abraham Lincoln

Philip Clark

More Wayland History Makers

First published in 1981 by Wayland Publishers Ltd
49 Lansdowne Place, Hove, East Sussex BN3 1HF, England

© Copyright 1981 Wayland Publishers Ltd
ISBN 0 85340 814 9

Typeset by Computacomp (UK) Ltd, Fort William, Scotland
Printed in Italy by G. Canale and C.S.p.A., Turin

Contents

Introduction

In January 1981, President Ronald Reagan gave his inaugural speech. As is the custom on these occasions, he paid tribute to his famous predecessors. When he came to President Lincoln, Reagan said, 'Whoever would understand in his heart the meaning of America will find it in the life of Abraham Lincoln.'

This view is shared by many citizens of the United States. One aspect of Lincoln's continuing appeal is the fact that he was entirely self-made. His family were pioneers of the Old West. His grandfather was killed by an Indian, and his father was one of the original 'sodbusters' (poor farmers who cleared virgin prairie in order to create farmlands). Lincoln achieved the highest office in the land through his own unaided efforts. Even more remarkably, he maintained, throughout his life, the personal integrity that earned him the nickname of 'Honest Abe'.

Abraham Lincoln's appearance is better known than that of any other American in history, except perhaps George Washington. William Howard Russell, of the London *Times*, remarked of Lincoln that 'It would not be possible for the most indifferent observer to pass him in the street without notice.' He was exceptionally tall, and the battered top hat, in which he often carried important papers, made him look even taller. His clothes always had a look of the second-hand about them, even when, as President, he took trouble with his appearance.

'Lincoln was a supreme politician. He understood politics because he understood human nature.'
Charles A. Dana.

Lincoln talking to McClellan in the General's tent close to the battlefield at Antietam. The President paid a visit to his Commander-in-Chief in October 1862, having become exasperated by what he called McClellan's 'slows'.

Lincoln's face was so grained and leathery that people began to call him 'old Abe' when he was scarcely thirty years old. Since photography had been invented before Lincoln became famous, we know exactly what he looked like. However, photography at the time was a slow process. This is why Lincoln usually looks so sad in his photographs. His contemporaries agreed that when he began to speak, his homely features 'brightened, like a lit lantern'.

Certainly, much of Lincoln's fame rests on the fact that the period of his Presidency almost exactly coincided with the duration of the American Civil War. The fundamental causes of the war are rooted in American history. To some extent, the war was a conflict between two different lifestyles — the commercial and industrial way of life in the North, and the agricultural and plantation society of the South. The Southern way of life was built upon slavery: the Southerners believed that, once slavery was abolished, their way of life would go with it. The First Battle of Bull Run was described at the time as a contest between 'Southern *chivalry* and Northern *shovelry*'.

Was the Civil War inevitable? As President, Lincoln had taken an oath to 'preserve, protect, and defend the Constitution of the United States.' The way he saw it, Lincoln could not recognize the right of individual states to leave the Union. However, to the Southerners he said, 'In *your* hands my dissatisfied fellow-countrymen, and not in *mine*, is the momentous issue of civil war. The government will not assail *you*. You can have no conflict, without being yourselves the aggressors.'

It is difficult to see how Lincoln could have taken a middle course between recognizing the Confederate States or civil war. Pledged as he was to preserve the

'... I am loth to close. We are not enemies, but friends. We must not be enemies. Though passion may have strained, it must not break our bonds of affection. The mystic chords of memory, stretching from every battle-field, and patriot grave, to every living heart and hearthstone, all over this broad land, will yet swell the chorus of the Union, when again touched, as surely they will be, by the better angels of our nature.'
Conclusion of Lincoln's first inaugural speech.

Union, Lincoln firmly believed that he had no choice at all. A different president might perhaps have backed down: given Lincoln's views, however, from the moment of his election, war between North and South was almost inevitable.

At first, Lincoln's war aim was to preserve the Union, with the abolition of slavery as the secondary issue. However, as it progressed, Lincoln seems to have come under pressure to turn the war into one to end slavery. The anti-slavery issue changed the war into a kind of crusade, and helped to prevent countries in other parts of the world from recognizing, and perhaps aiding, the Confederate States.

Part of Lincoln's greatness lay in his ability to combine doing what seemed to him to be right, with the political skills which ensured that he got his own way. There was more to 'Honest Abe' than met the eye. One verdict on him was that, 'While guilty of no

An historic photograph of President Lincoln delivering his second inaugural address at the Capitol on 4th March 1865. His tall figure (behind the speaking stand) towers over his contemporaries, many of whom are former Civil War generals.

Slavery was the basic issue that divided the Northern and Southern states. These freed slaves had worked on a plantation in South Carolina.

duplicity, he could hide his thoughts and intentions more efficiently than any man with a historical record.' A lawyer friend once said that he 'was harmless as a dove, and wise as a serpent.'

Lincoln was famous for his story-telling, a gift that he inherited from his father. He had a knack of getting at the truth in homely parables, and he could usually find an anecdote to fit any occasion. At one meeting, Lincoln and his Cabinet were discussing the wording of the Emancipation Proclamation. Secretary of State William H. Seward first suggested one change in the wording, then later suggested another. Lincoln recounted how Seward reminded him of a farm-hand out West, who informed the farmer that one of a yoke of oxen had dropped dead, adding after a pause, that the other ox had dropped dead too. When asked why he hadn't just said that both oxen were dead, he replied 'Because, I didn't want to hurt you by telling you too much at one time.' Lincoln often used tales like this to illustrate his points and keep his audiences amused.

During the Civil War, a friend once told Lincoln not to joke in the face of so much death and destruction. 'Don't you see?' he replied, 'If I didn't laugh, I would have to weep.'

'You have heard the story, haven't you, about the man who was tarred and feathered and carried out of town on a rail? A man in the crowd asked him how he liked it. His reply was that if it was not for the honour of the thing, he would much rather walk.'
Lincoln to a friend from Springfield who asked him how he liked being President of the United States.

1 'Pretty Pinching Times'

Abraham Lincoln was descended from an English family that had settled in Virginia just before the War of Independence. His grandfather and namesake had been a captain in the Virginia militia. In 1782, Abraham Lincoln the elder moved with his family westward to Kentucky. One of his children, Tom, was to be the father of the sixteenth President of the United States.

A couple of years later, Abraham Lincoln senior was working in a field with his sons when a shot rang out. Abraham fell to the ground and an Indian raced out of the woods and stood over the body. Then the six-year-old Tom saw the Indian fall, shot by another son, Mordechai Lincoln.

Lincoln's early life was spent in the frontier state of Kentucky, where life was hard and food had often to be hunted or gathered in the woods.

Lincoln's father 'removed to what is now Spencer County, Indiana, in the autumn of 1816. .... This removal was partly on account of slavery; but chiefly on account of the difficulty of land titles.'
Abraham Lincoln.

A 'blab school' similar to the one which Abe and his elder sister Sarah attended.

Tom Lincoln grew to manhood and learned the rudiments of carpentry. Like many others of his generation, he worked at a variety of trades: he was part-artisan, part-farmer and part-trader. On 12th June 1806, he married Nancy Hanks. Their first child, Sarah, was born the following year.

In 1808, Tom and his family moved to a farm at Nolin Creek, near Hodgenville, Kentucky. There he built a log cabin. It was in this log cabin that a son was born on Sunday, 12th February 1809. He was named Abraham after his grandfather. The baby was given to Dennis Hanks, his nine-year-old cousin, to hold. Dennis, who in later life had many interesting stories to tell about Lincoln's early years,

The log cabin in which Lincoln lived as a young boy.

handed the child back with the words, 'He'll never come to much.'

When young Abe Lincoln was two, the family moved to another farm nearby, at Knob Creek. The following year, another child, Thomas, died a few days after birth. Soon afterwards, Abe and Sarah began their schooling at the local 'blab school'. (These schools were so called because the children were made to repeat their lessons out loud.) Here, Abe would have learned to count and how to write the letters of the alphabet, in a primitive schoolhouse not unlike the log cabin that was his home.

The law in Kentucky at this time was still rough and ready, and Tom Lincoln had problems proving that the land he had paid for actually belonged to him. It may have been because of these land difficulties experienced by his father that Abraham made his eventual decision to study law. In 1816, Tom Lincoln decided to move north to Indiana.

After a long, hard journey, often hacking their way through the trackless wilderness, the family settled at a spot near Little Pigeon Creek, not far

'... it is a great piece of folly to attempt to make anything out of me or my early life. It can all be condensed into a single sentence, and that sentence you will find in Gray's Elegy: "The short and simple annals of the poor." '
Lincoln to John L. Scripps of the Chicago Tribune.

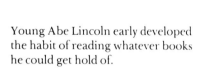

Young Abe Lincoln early developed the habit of reading whatever books he could get hold of.

from the Ohio River. There, they built a 'half-faced camp', which was a cabin with three walls. Instead of a fourth wall, a wood fire was kept burning night and day. The family lived on what they could shoot or gather in the woods — meat from bears, deer and wild turkeys; nuts, fruit and wild honey. As Abe was to put it later, they were 'pretty pinching times'.

On 8th October 1818, Nancy Hanks Lincoln died at the early age of 34, from what was then called the 'milk sick' (it was believed that the disease was caused by drinking poisoned milk). Soon afterwards, Abe was kicked by a horse and lay unconscious for many hours. He soon recovered, however, apparently none the worse for his experience.

The following year, Tom Lincoln made an expedition to Elizabethtown, Kentucky and returned with a new wife, Sarah Bush Johnston, a widow with three children of her own. There were now a total of eight people living in the primitive cabin.

From time to time Abe went to school at Pigeon Creek, but what he learnt from his schoolmasters was little compared with what he taught himself. He began to read everything he could lay his hands on. 'I never seen Abe after he was twelve 'at he didn't have a book some 'eers round', recalled Dennis Hanks. The only book in the cabin was the family Bible, but Abe managed to get hold of copies of Bunyan's *Pilgrim's Progress*, Defoe's *Robinson Crusoe*, Weems' *Life of George Washington*, and many others. These were some of the influences that helped to shape the prose style of the man who was to deliver the Gettysburg Address — probably the best-known speech in American history.

After the death of Abraham's mother when he was ten years old, his father married a widow — Sarah Bush Johnston. Abe was very fond of his stepmother.

'The things I want to know are in books; my best friend is the man who'll git me a book I ain't read.'
Abe Lincoln, as recalled by Dennis Hanks.

2 The Rail Splitter

Young Abe Lincoln grew to be exceptionally tall and strong. His height was 1.9 metres (6 ft 4 in). His arms and wrists were so strong that he could hold an axe out horizontally by the end of its handle, even at the end of his life. When he was eighteen he did all kinds of work for neighbouring farmers, but in later life it was for splitting rails to make fencing that he was best remembered. His active interest in law dates from this period, and he would often go into the courthouse to hear the lawyers speak.

In 1828, when Lincoln was nineteen, a farmer called James Gentry hired him to take a cargo of goods down the Mississippi River to New Orleans. Abe built a flatboat (a kind of raft). Then he and Gentry's son Allen set off on the long journey. Between Baton Rouge and New Orleans, a band of blacks tried to steal their cargo. Both Abe and Allen were injured in the fight that followed, but they managed to save their goods. Abe spent a few days in the bustling, cosmopolitan port of New Orleans before returning up the Mississippi by steamboat.

In 1830, a couple of weeks after Lincoln's twenty-first birthday, the family moved again, this time westward to Illinois. The journey, according to him, was 'slow and tiresome'. There followed the now familiar routine of selecting a site, building a cabin, and clearing a few acres of virgin prairie for farmland.

This was also the year of Lincoln's first political speech, when he got to his feet during a campaign

'Pants rolled up to the knees and shirt wet with sweat and combing his fuzzie hair with his fingers as he pounded away on the boat.'
Erastus Wright's description of Lincoln building the flatboat in 1831.

Opposite Abraham Lincoln — 'The Rail Splitter'. A neighbour recalled that 'Abe could sink an axe deeper into wood than any man I ever saw'.

On two occasions Lincoln was hired to take a cargo of goods in a flatboat down the Mississippi to New Orleans.

'My little dog jumped out of the wagon and the ice being thin he broke through and was struggling for life. I could not bear to lose my dog, and I jumped out of the wagon and waded waist deep in the ice and water, got hold of him and helped him out and saved him.'
From Lincoln's account of the family's journey to Illinois in 1830.

meeting in Decatur. When the family moved yet again the following spring, he did not go with them. Instead, he undertook a second Mississippi flatboat trip, this time with a cousin, John Hanks, and a stepbrother, John D. Johnston. Once more in New Orleans, Lincoln could see the slave trade at first hand as black men, women and children were bought and sold as though they were cattle.

Back in Illinois, Lincoln was given a job as clerk in charge of a store in New Salem owned by Denton Offutt, the man who had hired him for the Mississippi trip. Offutt had a bet with a neighbour that Lincoln could beat Jack Armstrong, a local wrestling champion. Lincoln won the bout, and thereby gained a reputation as a wrestler and athlete of considerable ability.

During this period, Lincoln continued his reading. He was not a very enthusiastic store clerk, and he usually had a book in his pocket. But he was now also starting to read law books in his spare time, and with the help of a lawyer friend was learning to draw up some of the simpler legal documents.

Lincoln was also taking his first, tentative steps into politics. He announced that he was running as a Whig candidate for the Illinois State Government. However, his political plans were dramatically interrupted. In the spring of 1832, the aged Indian war chief, Black Hawk, led a rising against the white settlers. Lincoln immediately volunteered to join the militia, and was promptly elected captain of a company by the men. He said later that nothing in his life ever gave him quite so much satisfaction again.

'In less than a year Offutt's business was failing — had almost failed — when the Black Hawk war of 1832, broke out.'
Abraham Lincoln.

A slave auction in New Orleans. According to John Hanks, Lincoln watched an auction and left saying, 'By God, boys, let's get away from this. If I ever get a chance to hit that thing (slavery), I'll hit it hard.'

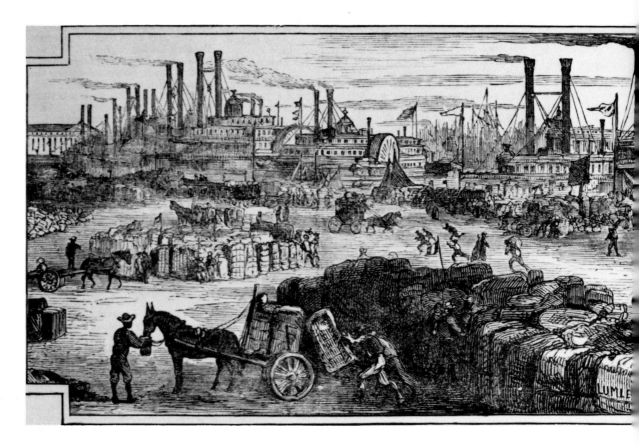

The busy cosmopolitan port of New Orleans, at the mouth of the Mississippi river.

Lincoln found the untrained men extremely difficult to lead. On one occasion some of them got drunk, and their captain was punished by being made to wear a wooden sword for two days. The war came to an end with the capture of Black Hawk, and Lincoln was discharged after eighty days' service.

Lincoln was not elected to the Illinois State Government that summer, and for a while he was without a job. Then he joined forces with a merchant called William F. Berry to run a general store. Business was slow, and Lincoln whiled away the time with his law books. In 1833 he also became part-time Postmaster of New Salem, at a salary of

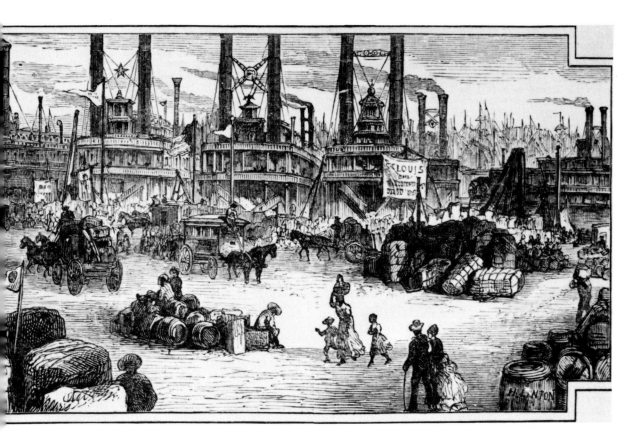

$50 a year.

In January 1835 Berry died suddenly, leaving Lincoln to settle his debts. These amounted to the then enormous sum of $1,100, and this debt was to hang round Lincoln's neck like a millstone for many years before, slowly and painfully, he paid it off.

'I — am — a man — and you — are another ... I took up the hatchet to avenge injuries which could not longer be borne ... I say no more of it; all is known to you.'
Chief Black Hawk to President Andrew Jackson.

3 The Young Lawyer

In 1833, Lincoln was offered a part-time job as a surveyor — a profession about which he knew very little. For some weeks he studied manuals about the subject deep into the night and soon he became known throughout the district as an accurate surveyor. He did not, however, lose his political ambitions. The following year, he again entered his name as a Whig candidate for the Illinois State Government elections.

This time, Lincoln was elected, coming second out of thirteen candidates for Sangamon County (a district of Illinois). At that time, the state capital of Illinois was Vandalia, about 120 kilometres (75 miles) from New Salem. In November 1834, Lincoln travelled to Vandalia. Here, he met the man who in time to come would be one of his most powerful political opponents, Stephen A. Douglas.

When the session ended in February, Lincoln returned to New Salem to his surveying and his law books. At this period, he seems to have formed an attachment to a Miss Ann Rutledge. This is one of those episodes in Lincoln's life where it is hard to separate the truth from the legend. According to some stories, Lincoln was actually engaged to Ann Rutledge. However, she died on 25th August 1835 and some contemporaries said that he took her death very hard and was never quite the same man again.

In December, Lincoln once again took the stage coach to Vandalia. As members of the state legislature were elected for two years only, he put

Opposite The earliest known photograph of Lincoln, taken when he was practising law in Springfield.

A notice in the *Sangamo Journal* announcing the first of Lincoln's law partnerships.

'My Father's life was of a kind which gave me but little opportunity to learn the details of his early career. During my childhood and early youth he was almost constantly away from home, attending courts or making political speeches. ...'
Robert Todd Lincoln.

himself forward for re-election the following August. This time, his name stood first among seventeen candidates. The Whigs of Sangamon County were all so tall — Lincoln was the tallest — that they were nicknamed the 'Lone Nine'.

The year 1836 marked another milestone in Lincoln's career. He passed his law examination, and later obtained a licence which enabled him to practise law in any of the courts of Illinois.

In the next session of the state parliament, Lincoln was one of the main supporters of a bill to move the capital of Illinois from Vandalia to Springfield. Another important issue was that of slavery. The Assembly passed resolutions in support of slavery in the so-called 'Slave States'. Lincoln and five others signed a note of protest that included the words, 'the undersigned ... believe that the institution of slavery is founded on both injustice and bad policy ...'

In 1837, Lincoln embarked on the first of a series of law partnerships, when he went into practice with J. T. Stuart. He then had a half-hearted love affair with a lady called Mary Owens. He appears to have proposed marriage to her, and to have been greatly relieved when, not surprisingly, she turned him down.

In 1840, Lincoln became engaged to Mary Todd, who as a girl used to tell her friends that her future husband would be President of the United States. (A former rival for her affection had been the politician Stephen A. Douglas.) One of Lincoln's law partners, William Herndon, told of the planned wedding. According to Herndon, the date was set for 1st January 1841. Everything was ready; the guests were present, the supper prepared. Even the bride was waiting. Only the bridegroom failed to turn up.

Whatever the truth of this story, there is no doubt that the engagement was broken off, and Lincoln later referred to that 'fatal 1st of January, 1841'. However, friends brought Lincoln and Mary together again, and they were finally married on 4th November 1842. The marriage was not an especially happy one. Mary was extravagant and ran up large bills for clothes. Nevertheless she was devoted to her husband and eager to make him happy. After a time, her behaviour became distinctly strange and she showed signs of mental instability. She used to shut herself up in her room for days on end, particularly after the death of her third son, Willie, in 1854.

Mary was often very difficult to get on with and would sometimes quarrel with servants and tradespeople. However, her life had not been easy. Three of her sons died young, and for much of their married life Lincoln was away from home. When Mary's husband became President, she had to share with him the severe strain of four years of civil war, during which three of her brothers were killed. Lincoln's behaviour, when he was with her in public, was patient and long-suffering. On one occasion, when she rounded on him in front of company, he walked away, 'hiding his face that others might not see it.'

After her husband's death, Mrs Lincoln's mind, never stable, became quite deranged, and for a time she was declared to be insane.

The Lincolns had four sons. The eldest, Robert Todd Lincoln, was born in 1843. He was the only one of the four to live to manhood but he was never close to his father. Edward Baker Lincoln (Eddie) was born in 1845 and died at the age of four. William Wallace Lincoln (Willie) born in 1850, died in 1862: Lincoln, as President, was almost prostrated by grief at Willie's death. Thomas (Tad) Lincoln was born in 1853. He was his father's favourite son; he outlived Lincoln but was still to die young in 1871.

Mary Todd whom Lincoln married in 1842. This photograph was taken before the ball given to celebrate her husband's inauguration.

4 Congressman Lincoln

In 1841, Lincoln and Stuart ended their legal partnership, and Lincoln joined forces with Stephen T. Logan. A law student named William H. Herndon was a junior member of the firm. After Herndon passed his bar exam, Lincoln started his own firm and offered Herndon a partnership. The two became lifelong friends, and their partnership lasted until 1861, when Lincoln was inaugurated as President.

After Lincoln's death, Herndon devoted the rest of his life to collecting information about Lincoln's early years. As a result, much of interest that would otherwise have been lost, has been preserved for Lincoln biographers. Unfortunately, much of Herndon's material is unreliable, and it is sometimes difficult to distinguish fact from fiction. But even Herndon, who once boasted that he knew his law partner better than Lincoln did himself, also stated that he could be the 'most shut-mouthed man' that ever lived.

Lincoln was an ambitious man. 'His ambition,' said Herndon, 'was a little engine that knew no rest.' Lincoln decided to run for a seat in the House of Representatives, the lower of the two houses of the United States Congress in Washington. In August 1846, he was duly elected to Congress, although he would not take office until the following year. This was a period of rapid expansion for the United States. Most of the great territory of Oregon on the west coast, which had been jointly occupied with

'I put it in my old hat, and buying a new one the next day, the old one was set aside, and so, the letter lost sight of for a time.'
Lincoln writing to a fellow lawyer explaining the temporary loss of a letter.

'The enduring power of Mr Lincoln's brain is wonderful. He can sit and think without food or rest longer than any man I ever met.'
William H. Herndon.

Opposite Lincoln was always ambitious. He decided to run for Congress and was duly elected in 1846.

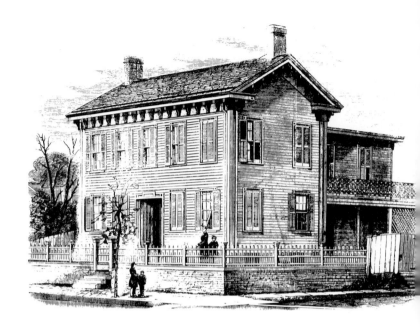

'His awkward gesticulations, the ludicrous management of his voice and the comical expression of his countenance, all conspired to make his hearers laugh at the mere anticipation of the joke before it appeared.'

From a newspaper account of one of Lincoln's speeches in 1848.

Right The Lincolns' house in Springfield, where they lived until they moved to Washington. This was the only house that Lincoln ever owned. He paid $1500 for it.

Below Chained together, a 'coffle' (gang) of slaves makes its way past the Capitol in Washington.

Britain, was acquired by treaty. At about the same time, the United States went to war with Mexico over a boundary dispute. One of the issues was that Mexico had freed her slaves in 1827, but her northern province of Texas refused to do so, and had declared its independence. The Mexicans were defeated by the U.S. Army in a series of battles, and were forced to surrender.

Lincoln joined the Whigs in denouncing the Mexican war as unnecessary. This made him unpopular in Illinois, where majority opinion was behind the war. Mexico had to give up huge territories to the United States, including the present-day state of California and part of New Mexico. However, one result of the war was to emphasize the problems of slavery in the newly-won territories.

Lincoln's term in Congress ended in 1849, and he did not seek re-election. He failed to get a job as

Commissioner of the General Land Office. Instead, he was offered the post of Secretary of the Territory of Oregon, which he turned down.

Lincoln had made no particular mark as a politician, and it seemed that back in Springfield at the age of forty, his political career was over. In his own words, 'From 1849 to 1854, both inclusive, (Lincoln) practised law more assiduously than ever before.' His lawyer's practice thrived. Much of his work involved travelling in a horse-drawn buggy across the prairie between law courts, but Lincoln enjoyed it. One day he mentioned to Herndon that he had finally paid off the last of the debts he had incurred in his partnership with Berry.

In September 1847, the victorious U.S. Army, under General Winfield Scott, entered Mexico City. Many of Scott's officers were later to win fame as Civil War commanders.

5 The Douglas–Lincoln Debates

Stephen Douglas (nicknamed the 'Little Giant') was the leading Democrat in Illinois. He was also Lincoln's most formidable opponent.

In the autobiographical sketch quoted at the end of the last chapter, Lincoln continued, 'I was losing interest in politics when the repeal of the Missouri Compromise aroused me again.'

The Missouri Compromise dated from 1821. At the time that Missouri was admitted to the Union as a slave state, it was agreed that, in all the rest of the territory bought from France in the Louisiana Purchase, slavery should be prohibited north of latitude 36° 30' North.

To understand the significance of the Missouri Compromise, it is necessary to go back in history. The first shipload of African slaves was landed in Virginia in 1619. In the early days the staple crop of the Southern states was tobacco. Profits were so small that landowners were only able to prosper if their plantations were worked by the unpaid labour of black slaves. Then the Industrial Revolution in England produced a demand for cotton that could be made into cheap clothing by the new spinning and weaving machines. But what really revolutionized the economy of the Southern states was the invention of the cotton gin (engine) in 1793 by Eli Whitney. This machine could remove the seeds from cotton much faster than could be done by hand. Huge cotton plantations grew in the South, and many thousands of slaves were needed to work them.

The Northern states became increasingly industrialized, and had little need for slave labour, which they eventually abolished. From this point onwards, new states were admitted to the Union in pairs — one slave and one free state. One aspect of the Missouri Compromise was a Fugitive Slave Law that stated that a slave who had escaped to a free state had to be returned to his owner. Opponents of slavery organized an 'Underground Railroad' to help escaped slaves get to Canada, where slavery was illegal.

The agent of the repeal of the Missouri Compromise was Lincoln's old rival, Senator Douglas. His Kansas-Nebraska bill proposed the division of the territory of Nebraska into two new states, Kansas and Nebraska. It was expected that Kansas would become a slave state and Nebraska a free state.

The Kansas-Nebraska bill provoked a storm of protest in the North. Opponents of the bill pointed out that it was likely to result in slavery being introduced in new states and territories — the opposite to the spirit of the Missouri Compromise.

Lincoln joined in the protest. One of his best-known speeches was delivered in Peoria on 16th October 1854, and is known as the 'Peoria Speech'. In this speech, Lincoln set out his position. He accepted the right of the Southern states to hold slaves, but he was determined to stop the spread of slavery to the new territories.

Whig opponents of slavery were now joining the new Republican party in increasing numbers, and in the spring of 1856 Lincoln did likewise. At a Republican convention, Lincoln delivered his so-called 'Lost Speech'. 'Unless ... a change is made in our present course, blood will flow on account of Nebraska, and brother's hand will be raised against

'We will say to the Southern disunionists, *We* won't go out of the Union, and you *shan't*.'
From Lincoln's 'Lost Speech', as recalled by William Herndon.

Slaves working a cotton gin on a Southern plantation. The invention of this machine dramatically increased the demand for slave labour.

The North had become heavily industrialized, and could rely on machines instead of slave labour.

'I take it for granted that the present question is a mere preamble — a title page to a great tragic volume.'
John Quincy Adams.

brother!' The effect of Lincoln's oratory on his audience was electric. Newspaper reporters, who should have been taking notes, clustered around Lincoln, spellbound. As a result, there is no authentic text of the speech — hence its name. Afterwards, a delegate called William Hopkins exclaimed, 'Lincoln, I never swear, but that was the damnest best speech I ever heard.'

In June, Lincoln was nominated as Republican Vice-Presidential candidate, though he was not elected. Then, on 7th March 1857, the United States Supreme Court delivered a judgement on the case of a black slave named Dred Scott. Scott's claim was

The work of the slave gangs was supervised by white overseers, who often carried whips.

that he was a free man because he had been taken to live in states where slavery was illegal. Chief Justice Taney ruled that slaves were property, and could therefore be taken anywhere in the United States. There was an outcry at this decision, and Lincoln decided to do his utmost to have the judgement reversed.

In 1858, the Republican party nominated Lincoln as its 'first and only choice' to represent Illinois in the Senate. His Democratic opponent was Stephen Douglas, regarded by many of his fellow-countrymen as the greatest living orator in the United States. It is thus a great tribute to Lincoln's

Lincoln 'rose from his seat, stretched his long, bony limbs upward as if to get them into working order, and stood like some solitary pine on a lonely summit.'
Francis Grierson.

Above Lincoln, the 'stump orator', speaking at one of his open-air debates with Douglas.

Below Harriet Beecher Stowe, author of *Uncle Tom's Cabin*. This passionate attack on slavery had an enormous influence on anti-slavery opinion.

powers as a public speaker that he was chosen. In accepting the nomination, Lincoln delivered his celebrated 'House Divided' speech, which contained the biblical quotation: 'A house divided against itself cannot stand.'

In July, Lincoln challenged Douglas to a series of public debates at seven different locations in Illinois. Douglas accepted the challenge. Douglas charged Lincoln with wanting to abolish slavery altogether. Lincoln retorted that Douglas agreed with Chief Justice Taney's ruling that the Declaration of Independence — 'all men are created equal' — did not apply to blacks. Neither charge was quite accurate.

In the eyes of the public, the result of this contest between two men of great ability was a draw. In the event, Douglas was returned to the Senate. But the debates had attracted such nationwide attention that Lincoln had become a national figure. He was overwhelmed with invitations to give speeches, and many Republicans began to see him as a potential candidate for the Presidency in 1860.

6 The Republican Candidate

On 17th October 1859, an anti-slavery fanatic named John Brown and about twenty men seized the United States arsenal at Harper's Ferry, West Virginia. Brown's object was to start a slave revolt, and in this he failed. His men were all killed or captured by a force of eighty marines under Colonel Robert E. Lee. Brown himself was later hanged.

John Brown was injured during his unsuccessful attack on the arsenal at Harper's Ferry. He was executed for trying to start a slave revolt.

The hall built for the 1860 Republican Convention became known as 'The Wigwam'. It could hold 10,000 people.

Brown's action enraged the South, and Lincoln deplored it because Brown had acted illegally. Meanwhile, pressure was mounting on Lincoln to become the Republican Presidential candidate. At first Lincoln demurred. 'I must, in candor, say,' he wrote, 'I do not think myself fit for the Presidency. ...' However, as the pressure increased, Lincoln's tone began to change. In one letter he admitted, 'The taste *is* in my mouth a little. ...'

During 1859, Lincoln travelled a total of about 6,500 kilometres (about 4,000 miles) and gave twenty-three speeches. Then, on a snowy night in February

1860, he gave a speech at the Cooper Union, New York. He was slow getting started. 'Mr *Cheerman*,' he began, in his Kentucky drawl. Slowly, he warmed to his theme. Slavery was wrong, and because it was wrong, it must not be allowed to spread. Lincoln finished his speech by calling on Republicans to 'have faith that right makes might' and to have the courage to do their duty as they understood it.

At the Illinois State Republican convention on 9th May, John Hanks brought two fence rails that he and Lincoln had split in 1830. 'Identify your work!' cried the members of the convention. 'It may be that I split these rails,' replied Lincoln. Then he looked at them more closely. 'Well boys,' he added, 'I can only say that I have split a great many better-looking ones.' Lincoln was promptly dubbed 'the Rail Splitter' candidate.

Later in the same month came the real test at the Republican National Convention in Chicago. At the first ballot, William H. Seward of New York had 173 votes to Lincoln's 102. But as the minor candidates disappeared from the contest, Lincoln's share of the votes increased. In the final ballot, Lincoln obtained 364 of the 465 votes, and was duly elected Republican candidate for the Presidency.

During the subsequent Presidential campaign, Lincoln stayed in Springfield, leaving the campaigning to his managers, as was the custom. When the election came in November, he beat Douglas into second place on the popular vote. Even so, Lincoln had only a tiny share of the votes in the Southern states. This was an ominous sign. One remarkable aspect of Lincoln's election as President was that, unlike Douglas, he held no important public office at that time. In many other countries, he could not have been elected under these

A famous portrait of Lincoln which was painted during his election campaign.

'You can fool some of the people all of the time, and all of the people some of the time, but you can't fool all of the people all of the time.'
Lincoln to Milton Hay.

Jefferson Davis, an ex-soldier and former Secretary of War, was elected President of the Southern Confederate States.

circumstances. In Britain, for example, no one can serve as Prime Minister if they are not a member of either of the two Houses of Parliament.

Lincoln has left a description of his appearance at the time of the presidential campaign when he was aged fifty-one. 'I am,' he said, 'in height, six foot four inches, nearly; lean in flesh, weighing on an average one hundred and eighty pounds; dark complexion, with coarse black hair and gray eyes.' At this time of his life he made more of an effort to appear neat, but his clothes never looked as if they fitted properly. He wore long side-whiskers, but no beard. Then, an eleven-year-old girl wrote to him suggesting he should grow one. Lincoln did grow the beard, and became the first United States President to wear one. The face with the beard has become so familiar that in the earlier photographs he looks odd without it.

At the time that Lincoln was elected, the new President did not take office until March of the following year. The Southern states had been waiting impatiently for the result. As soon as the state government of South Carolina heard that Lincoln was to be President, it called a convention to decide whether or not to stay in the Union. In December, South Carolina announced that it had seceded (broken away) from the Union.

The Southern states were convinced, despite Lincoln's assurances, that the North intended to abolish slavery throughout the entire country. Most Southerners believed that their economic system depended on slavery and that it would collapse without it. For many Southern landowners slaves represented a bigger cash investment even than the land they worked.

Southerners also feared that bands of freed blacks

would rove through the country. For years they had been haunted by the fear of a slave revolt. Blacks made up more than a third of the total population of the Southern states. What would happen if they were all suddenly freed? The poorer whites were also worried by the prospect of free blacks working for low wages and competing for jobs.

During January and February 1861, six more Southern states — Mississippi, Florida, Alabama, Georgia, Louisiana and Texas — seceded from the Union. The seven states then held a convention at which they elected Jefferson Davis as their president. A number of other Southern states soon joined them, and thus the Confederate States of America was born.

Alarm in the South. This cartoon shows a Southern planter arming his slaves to resist invasion from the North.

'As I would not be a *slave*, so I would not be a *master*. This expresses my idea of democracy. Whatever differs from this, to the extent of the difference, is no democracy.'
Abraham Lincoln.

7 President Lincoln

On 11th February 1861, a special train carrying Lincoln and his party steamed out of Springfield. It was to be the last time Lincoln set foot there. His journey to the capital was a leisurely one, and as there had been threats to assassinate him, he arrived in Washington secretly on the morning of 23rd February.

Lincoln was sworn in as President on 4th March by the aged Chief Justice Taney. Lincoln looked behind him for somewhere to put his hat. Stephen Douglas took it from him with a smile. In his inaugural speech, Lincoln sought to calm some of the fears of the South, but declared emphatically that no state had the right to leave the Union.

The next day the Senate approved Lincoln's list of nominations for his cabinet. The two most significant appointments were the former Whig and Lincoln's close rival for the Presidential nomination, William H. Seward as Secretary of State, and the former Democrat, Salmon P. Chase as Secretary of the Treasury. The Secretary of War was Simon Cameron, and the Secretary of the Navy was the bearded and bewigged Gideon Welles.

Cameron proved to be inefficient, and in the following year was replaced by an abrasive lawyer called Edwin M. Stanton. Many years before, Stanton had met Lincoln when they were on the same side in a lawsuit, and commented, 'Where did that long-armed baboon come from?' Stanton continued to refer to Lincoln as the 'original gorilla', but he

'In *your* hands, my dissatisfied fellow countrymen, and not in *mine*, is the momentous issue of civil war. The government will not assail *you*. You can have no conflict, without being yourselves the aggressors. *You* have no oath registered in Heaven to destroy the government, while *I* shall have the most solemn one to preserve, protect and defend it.'
From Lincoln's first inaugural address.

Opposite President Lincoln, painted a year before his death. The familiar image on the U.S. five-dollar bill was engraved from this famous portrait.

Lincoln rode in an open carriage on his way to the Capitol for his first inauguration. The dome of the Capitol was still being built.

proved a much more efficient Secretary of War than Cameron.

By April, most of the Union's military positions within the Confederate states had been evacuated. The principal exception was Fort Sumter in Charleston Harbour, South Carolina. After considerable argument about the next move, Lincoln decided to try sending provisions to Fort Sumter. The commanding officer, Major Robert Anderson, had already indicated that he could not hold out for long without relief. The Confederates then demanded Anderson's surrender. He refused, and in the early morning of 12th April 1861, Confederate guns opened fire on Fort Sumter. The American Civil War had begun.

Anderson surrendered thirty-four hours after the bombardment had started. On 15th April, Lincoln appealed to the Northern states for 75,000 troops. Two days later, Virginia seceded from the Union. This development left the city of Washington dangerously exposed to attack. Communications with the Northern capital were broken, and for over a week Washington was virtually undefended. Then, on 25th April, to Lincoln's intense relief, troops did arrive, and Washington was temporarily safe again.

With the benefit of hindsight, it seems to us now that the South had no real hope of winning the war. But this was by no means obvious at the time; in fact many European observers thought the South would win. However, if we pause to draw up a 'balance sheet', the North began the war with many advantages. Supreme among these was a population of some 20 million, against the South's 5½ million whites and 3½ million slaves. Then came the fact that the North was much more highly industrialized — a vital factor in the supply of weapons and ammunition. Finally, the North had a much stronger navy, and this soon gave it command of the seas.

However, against these advantages the South began the war with much abler generals. It was only after a long process of trial and error that Lincoln was able to find skilful military commanders. Lincoln wanted Robert E. Lee, the most able commander in the United States, to lead the Northern forces. But Lee was a Virginian and he could not bring himself to fight his native state. Reluctantly, he threw in his lot with the Confederates. In June, the Confederates moved their capital from Montgomery, Alabama, to Richmond, Virginia, which was only about 160 kilometres (100 miles) from Washington.

'If Virginia stands by the old Union, so will I. But if she secedes (though I do not believe in secession as a constitution right, nor that there is sufficient cause for revolution) then I will still follow my native State with my sword, and, if need be, with my life.'
Robert E. Lee in a letter to General Winfield Scott.

Lincoln delivering his first inaugural address.

8 Civil War

The American Civil War can perhaps be regarded as the first modern war, in the sense that technology was a vital factor. Only seven years earlier, the Light Brigade had been charging down the wrong valley at Balaclava. But now, in addition to the big guns and the explosive shells used to wage this war, railways were utilized for the first time for the rapid transport of large numbers of troops, and Lincoln could usually keep in touch with his generals by telegraph.

Like all civil wars, the American Civil War divided families and friends. There were innumerable cases of fathers, sons and brothers fighting on opposite sides. The war aims of the two sides were also quite different. The South did not need to win, it merely needed to hold out until the North gave up. The North, on the other hand, had to force the Southern

The High Street, Richmond, Virginia, during the civil war. By the time the war had ended, much of the Southern capital lay in ruins.

states to rejoin the Union — a much harder task. Lincoln's objective was to bring the seceding states back into the Union. He did not go to war to prevent slavery, but in order to preserve the Union of all the states.

In July 1861, Lincoln, who as President was also Commander-in-Chief of the armed forces, ordered General McDowell to attack the Confederate forces near Bull Run Creek on the Potomac River. The First Battle of Bull Run took place on 21st July and many sightseers travelled from Washington to watch.

At first the battle went well for the Northern troops. Then Colonel Thomas J. Jackson brought up Confederate reinforcements and halted the retreat. Jackson was to become one of the greatest of the Confederate Generals. At Bull Run, someone remarked, 'There is Jackson standing like a stone wall,' and from then on he was always known as

Northern troops in full retreat after the First Battle of Bull Run. In the South, Bull Run was known as the Battle of Manassas.

On 9th March 1862, the North's ironclad *Monitor* joined battle with the victorious Confederate ironclad *Merrimac* at Hampton Roads. The Battle was the first ever encounter between armour-plated ships. It ended inconclusively, but never again did the South seriously challenge the North's naval supremacy.

'Lee is a phenomenon. He is the only man I would follow blindfold.'
General Stonewall Jackson.

Stonewall Jackson. Now it was time for the Union troops to retreat. Many of them continued retreating until they reached Washington.

Bull Run was proclaimed a Southern victory. But the Southerners threw their success away by their inability to follow it up, thus giving the Union forces time to reorganize. The following day, Lincoln appointed General George G. McClellan to be the commander of the army of the Potomac. McClellan was a good-looking man of thirty-four with a fine military record. He was a brilliant organizer, and much loved by his troops. In a short time, he converted the disorganized Army of the Potomac into a real army. But McClellan also had serious faults. Though personally brave, he was not a great combat general and he seemed incapable of fast movement of his troops.

Lincoln also had his political troubles. He had to get rid of General Frémont of Missouri, who had exceeded his authority by proclaiming military law in his state. But even more tricky was the *Trent* affair. The *Trent* was a British merchant ship that had been stopped by a U.S. warship. The American captain removed two Confederate officials from the *Trent*, and took them to Boston where they were imprisoned. The British government was outraged, and demanded that the two Confederates be released. The Union could easily have been involved in war with Britain, but Lincoln sensibly backed down, remarking 'One war at a time.'

As if Lincoln did not have enough troubles, personal tragedy struck him in February 1862. His little son Willie came back from riding his pony with a cold that rapidly turned to pneumonia. Death came soon afterwards, and Willie's parents were utterly grief-stricken. 'It is hard, hard, hard to have him die!' exclaimed Lincoln, with tears in his eyes.

Mary Lincoln would never again go into the Guest's Room in the White House, which was where her son had died.

Meanwhile, a previously unknown brigadier called Ulysses S. Grant was winning Union victories in the West. Grant forced a Confederate army of 14,000 men to surrender at Fort Donelson on the Cumberland River. This victory ensured that Kentucky, which might have gone over to the South, remained in the Union.

On the 6th April 1862, General Albert S. Johnston attacked Grant at Shiloh. After a bloody battle, in which Johnston was killed, Grant drove back the attackers. A rumour went around that Grant had

South Carolina troops campaigning in Missouri. Many of the Southern regiments fought for their state first, with the Confederacy a long way second.

47

The *Trent* Affair. The captain of the U.S. warship *San Jacinto* stopped the British mail steamer *Trent* and took off two Confederate officials. The affair almost involved the North in war with Britain.

allowed himself to be surprised because he was drunk. When efforts were made to remove him, Lincoln replied laconically, 'I can't spare this man — he fights!'

The North at this time had virtually no intelligence service. McClellan had to rely on detectives from the Pinkerton Detective Agency, who tended to greatly exaggerate the numbers of the enemy. The cautious General McClellan finally caught up with the Confederates at Yorktown, and settled down for a siege, only to find that the enemy had slipped away. At Williamsburg, McClellan's army clashed with the Confederates, who retreated towards Richmond.

Meanwhile, the Confederate General Stonewall Jackson was rampaging through the Shenandoah Valley. After winning several battles, Jackson threatened Washington itself. Lincoln was forced to recall troop reinforcements, on their way to McClellan, to defend the capital.

Jackson evaded all the Union armies sent in pursuit of him, and rejoined General Robert E. Lee, who was later appointed General-in-Chief of the Confederate armies. Lee and Jackson then attacked McClellan in the Seven Days' battles. The Union

army stood up well to this onslaught, and at the finish it was the Confederates that had to retire.

Lincoln now organized a new Army of Virginia, commanded by General John Pope. Pope's army was defeated by Jackson and Lee at the Second Battle of Bull Run in August. McClellan was reinstated, first as commander of the troops defending Washington, and later of all 'the forces in the field'.

Lee next decided to carry the war into Union territory. He led his armies across the Potomac into Maryland. On 17th September McClellan attacked Lee at Antietam Creek. After heavy losses on both sides, Lee retired across the Potomac. McClellan failed to follow him across the river and cripple the Confederate armies.

Left General McClellan has been much critized for his excessive caution, but Lee said later that McClellan was the Northern general that he feared most.

Right Thomas J. (Stonewall) Jackson was Lee's greatest subordinate. He was accidentally killed by his own men at the Battle of Chancellorsville.

9 The Road to Gettysburg

In September 1862, Lincoln issued his preliminary Emancipation Proclamation (the final version was published on New Year's Day). It declared that all slaves in rebel territory 'shall be then, henceforward, and forever free.' Many of Lincoln's supporters had urged him to hold back until victory was in sight. But by this time the war had acquired a moral aspect: Lincoln was now fighting a war, not just to preserve the Union, but to abolish slavery as well.

In October Lincoln went to see McClellan at his camp at Harper's Ferry. He was becoming more and more worried at the General's lack of activity. During the following months Lincoln's patience snapped. 'I said I would remove him if he let Lee's army get away from him, and I must do it. He has got the slows ...' This time McClellan's removal was permanent.

McClellan was replaced by General Ambrose E. Burnside, whose magnificent whiskers have given us the word 'sideburns'. Burnside was promptly trounced by Lee at Fredericksburg. Lincoln discarded Burnside in favour of General 'Fighting Joe' Hooker. The following May, Lee defeated Hooker at Chancellorsville. But this was a costly victory for the South, for during the battle Stonewall Jackson, Lee's most brilliant subordinate, was killed.

During the last weeks of 1862, Lincoln was alarmed by increasing tension in his cabinet between Seward and Chase. Chase felt that Seward had undue influence over the President. First Seward, then

General McClellan handing over command of the Army of the Potomac to General Burnside (right).

The Union and the Confederacy

FREE TERRITORIES

MINNESOTA

WISCONSIN

MICHIGAN

MAINE

VERMONT

N.H.

NEW YORK

MASS.

CONN

RHODE isl.

PENNSYLVANIA

Gettysburg ☆

NEW JERSEY

DELAWARE

MARYLAND

Washington

IOWA

ILLINOIS

INDIANA

OHIO

WEST VIRGINIA

Springfield ☆

KANSAS

MISSOURI

KENTUCKY

Richmond ★

VIRGINIA

TENNESSEE

N.CAROLINA

INDIAN TERRITORY

ARKANSAS

S.CAROLINA

Charleston Harbour ★

ALABAMA

GEORGIA

Montgomery ★

TEXAS

MISSISSIPPI

LOUISIANA

FLORIDA

	UNION STATES
	BORDER STATES
	CONFEDERATE STATES

Lincoln reading the Preliminary Emancipation Proclamation to his cabinet.

Lincoln with his favourite son 'Tad'.

Chase, wrote letters of resignation. Chase's letter gave Lincoln a way out of the problem and a means of keeping both men in his cabinet. 'I've got a pumpkin in each end of my bag,' he announced. (This was the way in which country farmers balanced their horse's load.) Lincoln then wrote to both men saying that he needed them in the cabinet and could not accept their resignations.

As the Union armies began to close in on the South, control of the Mississippi River became a vital factor. Grant was determined to capture the key town of Vicksburg. He settled down to a long siege: the garrison were reduced to eating rats and shoe leather. President Davis had ordered the Confederate commander to hold Vicksburg at all costs.

On 3rd June 1863, Lee began his second all-out drive north. His target was Harrisburg, but Lincoln feared he might aim for Washington. On 28th June, Hooker resigned and was immediately replaced by General George G. Meade. Meade was ordered to protect Washington and to seek out Lee. On 1st July, advance units of the two armies met at Gettysburg. Here was to be fought the decisive battle of the war. When Lee arrived, although short of ammunition, he decided to carry on the fight. The Union forces retreated from the town and dug themselves in. On the following day the Confederates attacked again, but failed to break the Union position. On 3rd July, Lee made his last throw. After a preliminary bombardment, Lee sent General Pickett and 15,000 men across a wide valley under murderous fire. (Pickett's Charge has often been compared to the advance of the French Imperial Guard at Waterloo. It was equally heroic, and it also just failed.) Some of the men actually broke through the Union lines, but there were too few of them left to hold their ground. Lee miraculously got his army across the Potomac and back to Virginia. The following day, Vicksburg, on the Mississippi, surrendered to Grant.

In November, a great national cemetery for the Union dead was dedicated at the battlefield of Gettysburg. Lincoln was invited to say a few words. The main speaker, Edward Everett, spoke for two

> 'If I knew what brand of whiskey he (Grant) drinks I would send a barrel or so to some other generals.'
> *Lincoln to Nicolay and Hay (his secretaries and future biographers).*

> 'I should be glad if I could flatter myself that I came as near to the central idea of the occasion, in two hours, as you did in two minutes.'
> *Everett to Lincoln the day after the Gettysburg Address.*

President Jefferson Davis signing acts of the Confederate Government by the roadside.

Lincoln delivering the Gettysburg Address. It received little attention at the time but is regarded today as one of the noblest speeches ever made. The full text is on page 65.

hours. Lincoln's speech lasted for little more than two minutes. It did not make much impression at the time, but Lincoln's address is now perhaps the best-known passage ever written by a citizen of the United States. It ends, '... we here highly resolve that these dead shall not have died in vain — that this nation, under God, shall have a new birth of freedom — and that government of the people, by the people, for the people shall not perish from the earth.'

One of many problems that beset the Union Army was that of desertion, for which the penalty was death. Many stories are told of Lincoln using his presidential powers to pardon soldiers sentenced to be shot. In one case, Lincoln signed a reprieve, saying, 'Well, I don't believe *shooting* will do him any good.' Army commanders complained that Lincoln's pardons were harmful to military discipline, but the President continued to intervene when he believed he was justified in doing so. In one case of a young soldier sentenced to death for sleeping on sentry duty, Lincoln remarked, 'I cannot consent to shooting him for such an act.'

Lincoln used to refer to the bundles of documents concerning 'cowardice in the face of the enemy' as his 'leg cases'. He explained this expression by saying that 'if Almighty God gives a man a cowardly pair of legs how can he help their running away with him?'

One general who was noted for his particular severity was Major General Butler. To him, Lincoln once sent the following order: 'Please suspend execution in any and all sentences of death in your Department until further orders.' On another occasion, a soldier under Butler's command was under sentence of death. When the soldier's old father came in tears to Lincoln to plead for his son's

life, Lincoln responded, 'By Jings, Butler or no Butler, here goes.' He wrote out an order that the soldier was not to be shot until further orders from the President. When the old man protested that this was not a pardon, Lincoln replied, 'Well my old friend, I see you are not very well acquainted with me. If your son never looks on death till further orders come from me to shoot him, he will live to be a great deal older than Methuselah.'

Above The Union army besieging Vicksburg. Lincoln said that if Grant captured the city, 'he is my man and I am his the rest of the war.'

Right The Battle of Gettysburg. Where the Confederates, under Lee, were narrowly defeated, but miraculously made their escape across the Potomac.

10 'Grant Was to Go for Lee'

General Ulysses S. Grant, the commander whom Lincoln at last found to lead the North to victory.

In September 1863, Lincoln prodded General Rosecrans in Tennessee into attacking the Confederate General Bragg at Chattanooga. Bragg counter-attacked at the equally exotically-named Chickamauga Creek. Only the steadiness of General George H. Thomas ('the Rock of Chickamauga') prevented a total rout of the Union forces.

Soon afterwards, Grant was appointed commander of all troops in the West, and he and General Thomas forced the Confederates out of their positions near Chattanooga. Bragg only just avoided capture and retreated with his army to Georgia.

Lincoln decided that Grant was the man he had been looking for in vain for so long. The rank of Lieutenant General was revived for Grant and he was put in charge of all the Union armies.

Grant decided to return westward before devoting his attention to the campaign in the East. Before leaving Washington, he put General William T. Sherman in command of the Western armies. Sherman's account of their strategy was contained in a single sentence. Grant 'was to go for Lee and I was to go for Joe Johnston.' Grant was determined to hit the enemy and go on hitting him, 'until by mere attrition, if in no other way, there should be nothing left of him'. (The idea of attrition is like a game of

The great Confederate general, Robert E. Lee, who time after time inflicted terrible damage on the union armies and extricated his troops despite the North's overwhelming numbers. He is seen here on his faithful warhorse 'Traveller'.

chess where one player has more pieces than the other. If both players lose pieces at the same rate, the one who started with more is bound to win.)

The year 1864 was the fourth of the Civil War, and was to be the last. In the Spring, Grant's army met Lee's in a densely wooded area of northern Virginia called the Wilderness. In forty-eight hours of fighting, Grant had lost 14,000 men. Grant's losses were always greater than Lee's, but the North had much greater reserves of men. By June, Grant's losses amounted to over 50,000.

In May, Sherman left Chattanooga for Atlanta, Georgia. General Joseph E. Johnston was forced out of his defensive positions back to Atlanta. In September, Sherman marched into the city. In the same month, the Confederate fleet was destroyed at Mobile Bay.

In June, Lincoln had been re-elected as the Republican Presidential candidate by a large majority. He faced a much tougher challenge in the

'(Grant) had ... rather a scrubby look. He had a cigar in his mouth, and rather the look of a man who did, or once did, take a little too much to drink ... a slightly seedy look, as if he was out of office and on half pay, nothing to do but hang around....'
Richard H. Dana.

'We sent over the mountains and brought Mr Grant, as Mrs Grant calls him, to manage (the army) for us; and now I guess we'd better let Mr Grant have his own way.'
Lincoln to Edwin M. Stanton.

Above Sherman's March to the Sea left a wide path of destruction through the South, but some slaves hailed him as a conquering hero.

November Presidential elections. His chief opponent was General McClellan, who had been adopted as the Democratic candidate. Lincoln was pessimistic about his chances of re-election: '... it seems exceedingly probable,' he wrote, 'that this Administration will not be re-elected.' Nevertheless, Lincoln was elected for a second term of office. If he had not been, the war might well have dragged on even longer than it did.

Soon after the election, Sherman set off on his famous 'March to the Sea' through Georgia. Sherman's advance left a broad swathe of destruction; burnt buildings, farms laid waste, railways wrecked. Sherman's action probably shortened the war, but it left a legacy of bitterness in the South. In December, Sherman wrote to Lincoln, 'I beg to present to you as a Christmas gift, the city of Savannah ...' In the same month, General Thomas completely destroyed one of the three remaining Confederate armies at Nashville, Tennessee.

The year 1865 opened with a personal triumph for Lincoln. The Thirteenth Amendment to the Constitution, which prohibited slavery altogether, was approved by Congress and sent to the states for their agreement. Lincoln may have been under

Right A typical Southern city after the Union troops had passed through.

Refugees from Atlanta, Georgia, after the city had been captured by Sherman.

pressure from the Republican Party and Congress to make the ending of slavery into one of his chief war aims. At all events, he now made the prohibition of slavery one of his conditions for ending the war and the Thirteenth Amendment dealt the death-stroke to the keeping of slaves.

On 4th March 1865, Lincoln delivered his second inaugural speech. In it, he saw the war as a kind of punishment: 'every drop of blood drawn with the lash shall be paid by another drawn with the sword...' Yet the tone was of a man looking forward to victory, and after victory towards binding up his country's wounds.

On 2nd April, Grant broke through Lee's defences at Petersburg. Lee was forced to evacuate Richmond, and the following day, the Union Army entered the Confederate capital. By 9th April, Lee's army was

'I propose to fight on this line if it takes all summer.'
Grant at Spotsylvania, May 1864.

59

Lee signing the surrender at
Appomattox. He was wearing his
full-dress uniform. All the rest of his
kit had been captured by Grant's
army.

surrounded. 'There is nothing left for me to do but
to go and see General Grant,' said Lee, 'and I would
rather die a thousand deaths.'

Lee met Grant in a house in Appomattox Courthouse village. Lee was wearing his best uniform;
Grant wore a dusty blouse — he apologized for his
appearance. He had come straight from the field, he
said, and hadn't had time to change. They talked
about the old days in the Mexican War, and Lee had
to bring Grant back to the point of the meeting.
Grant, sensibly, was generous with his surrender
terms. With the surrender of Lee's army the war was
virtually over.

11 'Now He Belongs to the Ages'

Lincoln's task was now to pick up the pieces left by the war, and rebuild the Union. Over half a million men had died in the war. These enormous losses caused feelings of bitterness and resentment throughout the United States, and most particularly in the South.

On Good Friday, 14th April 1865, Lincoln attended his last cabinet meeting. This ended with a decision to meet again the following Tuesday. In the evening, Lincoln and his wife went to see a play called *Our American Cousin*, at Ford's Theatre. The policeman assigned to guard the Presidential box had deserted his post, thus enabling a fanatical Southerner called John Wilkes Booth to enter the box. Booth, an actor by profession, shot Lincoln in the back of the head. He then made his escape by jumping on to the stage, breaking his ankle in the fall. Lincoln was carried to a house across the street. He died there the following morning. Edwin M. Stanton, the Secretary of War, pronounced the famous epitaph: 'Now he belongs to the ages.'

On 26th April, John Wilkes Booth was cornered in a barn in Bowling Green, Virginia. The barn was set on fire, and Booth was shot as he tried to escape. Later, three men and a woman were hanged as fellow conspirators.

Lincoln's body lay in state in the Capitol, before

'There are men in Congress ... who possess feelings of hate and vindictiveness in which I do not sympathize and can not participate ...'
Lincoln to Grant

Lincoln discussing peace prospects with two of his Generals, Sherman and Grant.

The assassination of Lincoln in a
box in Ford's Theatre, Washington,
by John Wilkes Booth.

being taken, by way of New York, on the long
journey back to Springfield, the city from which he
had travelled to lead the United States to victory.
Lincoln was buried on 4th May. By the end of the
month, the last Confederate army in the field had
surrendered.

Lincoln had been much criticized towards the end
of his life, but after his death he was mourned by
many in the South as well as in the North. On the
same day that Booth was shot, Johnston surrendered
his army to Sherman. Johnston remarked that
Lincoln's death was a tragedy for the South, and so it
was to prove.

Throughout the Civil War, Lincoln had held to the
view that the Southern states were so many 'Prodigal
Sons' who would eventually return to the Union. He
was critical of generals like Meade who referred to
the Confederates as 'invaders'. In this approach,
Lincoln was frequently at odds with Congress, which
took a much harder line.

Lincoln was succeeded as President by Vice-

President Andrew Johnson, whose attitude was typical of many sections of Congress. 'Treason is a crime,' stated Johnson, 'and must be punished as a crime.' However in May 1865 he issued a proclamation pardoning most of the former Confederates, although some of the Southern generals and politicians had to wait another three years for a full pardon.

Meanwhile, in some respects, the South was treated like a conquered country. It was divided into military districts, and many of the 'rebels' were stripped of their property and voting rights. The Southern states became a prime target for unscrupulous Northern politicians (called 'carpet-baggers') and others looking for plunder. As a result, many Southerners remained bitter towards the North for decades to come.

Lincoln's body was taken on a long funeral journey from Washington back to Springfield, Illinois. The engine is draped in black, and carries a large portrait of the dead President.

Above The funeral procession in Springfield. Many who criticized Lincoln's policies during his lifetime, joined in mourning his passing.

Right The text of Lincoln's immortal 'Gettysburg Address', delivered at the dedication of the national cemetery to the dead after the battle of Gettysburg.

Despite Lincoln's disagreements with Congress over the post-war treatment of the South, it is difficult to imagine that the Southern states would have been so badly treated if Lincoln had completed his second term of office. He was a realistic and flexible politician, skilled in getting his own way in the face of determined opposition.

Lincoln's speeches and writings have helped to form the tradition of modern democratic government, begun by such men as Thomas Jefferson, the main author of the Declaration of Independence. Lincoln did not belong to a particular church, but he exemplified the Christian virtue of loving his enemies. He was courageous in the face of danger and difficulty, and generous in victory. 'So long as I have been here,' he wrote the year before he died, 'I have not willingly planted a thorn in any man's bosom.'

'**F**OUR SCORE AND SEVEN YEARS AGO
our fathers brought forth on this continent, a new nation,
conceived in Liberty, and dedicated to the proposition that all
men are created equal.

Now we are engaged in a great civil war, testing whether
that nation, or any nation so conceived and so dedicated, can
long endure. We are met on a great battle-field of that war. We
have come to dedicate a portion of that field, as a final resting
place for those who here gave their lives that that nation might
live. It is altogether fitting and proper that we should do this.

But, in a larger sense, we can not dedicate — we can not
consecrate – we can not hallow — this ground. The brave
men, living and dead, who struggled here, have consecrated it,
far above our poor power to add or detract. The world will
little note, nor long remember what we say here, but it can
never forget what they did here. It is for us the living, rather, to
be dedicated here to the unfinished work which they who
fought here have thus far so nobly advanced. It is rather for us
to be here dedicated to the great task remaining before us —
that from these honored dead we take increased devotion to
that cause for which they gave the last full measure of devotion
— that we here highly resolve that these dead shall not have
died in vain — that this nation, under God, shall have a new
birth of freedom — and that government of the people, by the
people, for the people, shall not perish from the earth.'

*Abraham Lincoln at the dedication of the
cemetery at Gettysburg, Pennsylvania,
November 19, 1863*

Principal Characters

Booth, John Wilkes (1838–1865). Actor and assassin. Shot Lincoln at Ford's Theatre on 14th April 1865. Later caught and killed. His brother, Edwin Booth, was the foremost American actor of his time.

Brown, John (1800–1859). Anti-slavery fanatic. In 1859, he made an unsuccessful attempt to start a slave rebellion. Badly wounded and later hanged.

Burnside, Ambrose E. (1824–1881). Union general. Succeeded McClellan as Commander of the Army of the Potomac. Defeated by Lee at Fredericksburg in 1862.

Chase, Salmon P. (1808–1873). Lawyer and politician. Secretary of the Treasury in Lincoln's first administration. In 1864 became Chief Justice of the U.S. Supreme Court.

Davis, Jefferson (1809–1889). Soldier and politician. President of the Confederate States during the Civil War. Captured and imprisoned at the end of the war, but released two years later.

Douglas, Stephen A. (1813–1861). Politician. U.S. senator and a leader of the Democratic Party. A great opponent of Lincoln, Douglas nevertheless supported him after he had been elected President.

Grant, Ulysses S. (1822–1885). Union general and politician. In 1864, he was appointed Commander-in-Chief of the Union Army. He was elected President in 1868, and re-elected in 1872.

Hanks, Dennis. Lincoln's cousin who was his companion in his early days and remained in touch with him all his life — the only member of

Lincoln's family to visit him in the White House.

Herndon, William. Lincoln's junior partner in his law firm. Herndon was a lifelong friend of Lincoln's and their partnership lasted until his inauguration as president. After Lincoln's death, Herndon devoted his life to collecting information about his friend's early years.

Jackson, Thomas J. (1824–1863). Confederate general. Earned the nickname of 'Stonewall' Jackson after the First Battle of Bull Run. After winning a number of victories, he died of wounds received at Chancellorsville.

Lee, Robert E. (1807–1870). Confederate general. Considered by many to have been the greatest general on either side during the Civil War. After the war, Lee became President of Washington College, Virginia (now Washington and Lee University).

McClellan, George B. (1826–1886). Union general, and politician. Soon after the outbreak of war, Lincoln put him in charge of the Army of the Potomac, and later made him Commander-in-Chief. Relieved of his command in 1862, he ran unsuccessfully against Lincoln for President in 1864.

Meade, George G. (1815–1872). Union general. In July 1863, he beat the Confederates under Lee at Gettysburg.

Seward, William H. (1801–1872). Lawyer and politician. In 1838, became Governor of New York. In 1861, Lincoln appointed him Secretary of State.

Sherman, William T. (1820–1891). Union general. Famous for his 'March to the Sea' through Georgia in 1864.

Stanton, Edwin M. (1814–1869). Lawyer and politician. Appointed Secretary of War by Lincoln in succession to Simon Cameron.

Table of Dates

1859	John Brown seizes government arsenal at Harper's Ferry.
1860	Lincoln chosen as Republican Presidential candidate. Elected President, on 6th November.
1861	Formation of Confederate States of America. Lincoln inaugurated, 4th March. Outbreak of Civil War. Union defeat at the First Battle of Bull Run.
1862	Battle of Shiloh ending in costly victory for the North. Sherman's Shenandoah Valley Campaign and Lee's Seven Days Campaign. Second Battle of Bull Run — Union army defeated. Lee's army forced to retreat after Battle of Antietam. Burnside defeated at Fredericksburg.
1863	1st January Lincoln issues Emancipation Proclamation. Hooker defeated at Chancellorsville. Lee defeated at Gettysburg. Surrender of Vicksburg to Grant. Battles of Chickamauga and Chattanooga. 19th November Lincoln delivers *Gettysburg Address* at dedication of Gettysburg cemetery.
1864	Grant appointed Commander-in-Chief. Wilderness campaign. Lincoln re-elected as President.
1865	Lincoln inaugurated for second term. Sherman's March to the Sea. Battle of Nashville. Lee surrenders to Grant, 9th April. Lincoln shot by John Wilkes Booth, 14th April; dies the following day. 26th April, Booth caught and shot; Johnston surrenders to Sherman.

Further Reading

Bishop, Jim *The Day Lincoln Was Shot* (Weidenfeld, 1955).

Current, Richard *The Lincoln Nobody Knows* (McGraw-Hill, 1958).

Donald, David *Lincoln Reconsidered* (Knopf, 1956).

Fehrenbacher, Don E. *Prelude to Greatness: Lincoln in the 1850's* (Stanford University Press, 1962).

Hofstadter, Richard *The American Political Tradition* (Knopf, 1948).

Latham, Frank B. *Abraham Lincoln* (Franklin Watts, 1968).

Luthin, R. H. *The Real Abraham Lincoln* (Prentice-Hall, 1960).

Mitgang, Herbert *The Fiery Trial* (Viking, 1974).

Randall, J. G. *Lincoln the President* (4 volumes, Eyre & Spottiswoode, 1945).

Sandburg, Carl *Abraham Lincoln: The Prairie Years and The War Years* (Harcourt Brace, 1954).

Thomas, Benjamin P. *Abraham Lincoln* (Eyre & Spottiswoode, 1953).

Williams, T. Harry *The Union Sundered* (Time-Life Books, 1974).

Index

Picture acknowledgements

Mary Evans, front cover. B.B.C. Hulton Picture Library, frontispiece, 9, 11, 20–21, 26, 28, 28 (lower), 31, 34 (lower), 35, 37, 44, 46, 48, 49 (left), 52 (lower), 53, 54, 55 (upper and lower), 58 (upper); Mansell Collection, back cover, 30, 43, 49 (right), 56, 57; John Topham 16, 18, 40, 52 (upper), 61; Peter Newark's Western Americana 6, 10, 12, 13, 14, 15, 19, 22, 24, 25, 33, 38, 42, 55. Map on page 51 is by Malcolm Walker. Remaining pictures are from the Wayland Picture Library.